With Love, Me
Beauty in the Unexpected

A Journey of Compassion, Creativity, and Community with the Duchess of Sussex

TIFFANY C. KINGSBURY

COPYRIGHT

TABLE OF CONTENTS

INTRODUCTION

The Vision Behind "With Love, Meghan"

"With Love, Meghan" is more than a series; it is a heartfelt invitation to explore the intersections of compassion, creativity, and community. Meghan, the Duchess of Sussex, envisioned this project as a way to connect with people on a deeper level by sharing personal experiences, meaningful conversations, and practical advice. Rooted in her life's journey, the series emphasizes authenticity and the beauty of embracing imperfection.

This vision stems from Meghan's own experiences navigating challenges and opportunities as a global public figure, advocate, and mother. From her California roots to her royal platform, Meghan has consistently sought to use her voice and influence to uplift others.

Through "With Love, Meghan," she aims to inspire viewers to cultivate kindness, creativity, and joy in their own lives, regardless of their circumstances.

Embracing Playfulness Over Perfection

One of the central themes of the series is the idea of letting go of the pursuit of perfection. In a world that often glorifies unattainable standards, Meghan advocates for finding joy in the process rather than focusing on the outcome.

Whether it's rolling up her sleeves to cook a simple meal or getting her hands dirty in the garden, Meghan encourages viewers to approach life with curiosity and playfulness.

Her philosophy is a refreshing reminder that mistakes and imperfections are not failures but opportunities to grow, connect, and discover unexpected beauty. By sharing her own moments of vulnerability and imperfection, Meghan invites viewers to embrace their humanity and find contentment in the everyday.

This approach also aligns with Meghan's belief in the transformative power of creativity. From crafting to cooking, the series showcases how small acts of creation can bring joy, foster connections, and remind us of the resilience within ourselves and our communities.

A Royal Perspective on Compassion, Creativity, and Community

As a former actress, philanthropist, and royal, Meghan's life has been a tapestry of diverse experiences that inform her unique perspective. She has leveraged her platform to advocate for issues such as gender equality, racial justice, and mental health awareness, demonstrating that compassion can be a powerful catalyst for change.

"In With Love, Meghan," viewers will see how these values are interwoven into her everyday life. Meghan's perspective is deeply rooted in the idea that community begins with small, intentional acts of kindness and that creativity can be a unifying force.

From volunteering with her husband, Prince Harry, to sharing meals with evacuees, Meghan exemplifies how compassion and creativity can bring people together, even in times of crisis.

Her approach also reflects a modern interpretation of royal duties—one that prioritizes personal connection over pomp and circumstance. Meghan believes that everyone, regardless of status, has the ability to make a meaningful impact on the lives of others. Through this series, she hopes to inspire audiences to take small but significant steps toward building stronger, more compassionate communities.

By blending practical advice with heartfelt storytelling, "With Love, Meghan" sets the stage for a transformative journey. It is a celebration of humanity in all its messy, beautiful forms and a reminder that even the smallest acts of love can create ripples of change.

CHAPTER ONE

Roots of Compassion

Compassion is not an inherent trait; it is a seed that is planted, nurtured, and allowed to flourish through life experiences. For Meghan, the Duchess of Sussex, this seed was planted early in her life, growing in a unique blend of familial values, multicultural influences, and firsthand experiences in service to others.

This chapter explores how her upbringing, humanitarian efforts, and commitment to helping others laid the foundation for a life centered on empathy and action.

Growing Up in California: A Foundation of Empathy

Meghan's journey of compassion began in the vibrant, diverse neighborhoods of California. Growing up in Los Angeles, she was immersed in a multicultural environment that celebrated diversity but also highlighted systemic inequalities.

Her mother, Doria Ragland, played an instrumental role in fostering her sense of empathy and social awareness. As a social worker and yoga instructor, Doria instilled values of mindfulness, kindness, and service in her daughter from an early age.

Family discussions around the dinner table often centered on the importance of standing up for what is right and supporting those in need. These conversations were not just theoretical but backed by action.

Meghan recalls visiting soup kitchens and community centers with her mother, where she witnessed the profound impact of small acts of kindness on individuals and families.

The vibrant yet complex tapestry of California also exposed Meghan to the realities of social disparity. These experiences fueled her curiosity and motivated her to understand the stories of those around her.

Whether it was through volunteer work, school projects, or personal interactions, Meghan began to see that compassion was not just a feeling but a practice—one that could change lives.

Life Lessons from Humanitarian Work

Meghan's commitment to compassion extended beyond her childhood, becoming a defining aspect of her adult life. Her involvement in humanitarian work introduced her to global challenges and the resilience of people who face them daily.

In her early twenties, Meghan traveled to Rwanda as an ambassador for World Vision, witnessing the impact of clean water initiatives on local communities. This experience was transformative, showing her the importance of sustainable solutions and empowering women and children.

It also reinforced her belief that compassion must be paired with action to create meaningful change.

Her work with UN Women further deepened her understanding of gender equality and the systemic barriers women face worldwide.

Meghan's powerful speech on International Women's Day 2015, where she declared herself a feminist, underscored her commitment to amplifying the voices of marginalized groups.

These experiences shaped her worldview and strengthened her resolve to use her platform to advocate for others.

In addition to her global efforts, Meghan continued to engage with local communities. Whether volunteering at a homeless shelter or mentoring young girls, she demonstrated that compassion knows no boundaries—it can be as impactful in one's neighborhood as it is on a global scale.

Finding Purpose Through Helping Others

Meghan's life has been a testament to the idea that purpose is discovered through service. Her philanthropic journey has not only impacted countless lives but has also given her a sense of fulfillment and direction. By helping others, Meghan found clarity about her values and priorities, which shaped both her personal and professional choices.

Through her experiences, Meghan learned that compassion is a reciprocal act. While she provided support and advocacy, she also gained profound insights and inspiration from the people she served.

This exchange of humanity became a cornerstone of her purpose: to create spaces where stories could be shared, connections could be forged, and lives could be transformed.

Her marriage to Prince Harry amplified this mission. Together, they have focused on initiatives addressing mental health, social justice, and community empowerment. Their shared commitment to compassion is evident in their hands-on approach, whether visiting disaster-stricken areas, comforting evacuees, or collaborating with organizations like World Central Kitchen.

In “With Love, Meghan,” these foundational principles are woven into every episode. Meghan’s story of growing up with empathy, learning from global experiences, and finding purpose in helping others serves as an inspiring reminder that compassion is not a destination but a lifelong journey.

Through her lens, viewers are encouraged to reflect on their own roots of compassion and take steps to make a difference in their communities.

CHAPTER TWO

Love in the Kitchen

The kitchen is often called the heart of the home, and for Meghan, it has always been a place of connection, creativity, and love. In this chapter, we explore how cooking became a meaningful expression of care in Meghan's life, shaped by her personal experiences, humanitarian efforts, and collaborations with organizations like World Central Kitchen (WCK).

It also highlights her philosophy of using food as a tool for nurturing relationships, celebrating diversity, and fostering community.

Cooking with Heart: Simple Recipes for Connection

Cooking, for Meghan, has never been about elaborate meals or culinary perfection. Instead, it has always been about creating moments of connection. From her early days learning recipes with her mother to hosting friends and family at her home, Meghan embraced the idea that food is a universal language that brings people together.

In "With Love, Meghan," she shares simple, heartfelt recipes that anyone can recreate. These dishes are inspired by her multicultural upbringing in California, her travels around the world, and her love for experimenting in the kitchen.

From comforting soul food to vibrant salads with fresh, local ingredients, Meghan's recipes are less about following rigid instructions and more about infusing meals with personal touches and care.

Meghan's approach to cooking is refreshingly playful and forgiving. She encourages viewers to embrace the imperfections—burnt edges, uneven slices, or an unplanned substitution—reminding them that the joy of cooking lies in the process, not just the result.

Each recipe comes with a story or memory, illustrating how food has been a constant source of comfort and connection in her life.

Lessons from World Central Kitchen (WCK)

Meghan's work with World Central Kitchen (WCK), founded by Chef José Andrés, has profoundly influenced her perspective on the power of food to heal and unite. WCK's mission to provide meals in the wake of disasters aligns perfectly with Meghan's belief in food as an act of compassion.

During visits to disaster-stricken areas, Meghan witnessed how WCK's efforts went far beyond simply feeding people—they provided hope, stability, and a sense of community in times of crisis. She was deeply moved by the dedication of WCK's volunteers, who worked tirelessly to ensure that everyone, from evacuees to emergency workers, felt seen and cared for.

In this chapter, Meghan reflects on key lessons she learned from WCK:

The Power of Simplicity: Often, the most comforting meals are the simplest ones, prepared with love and intention.

The Importance of Community: Food is more than sustenance; it is a way to bring people together and rebuild a sense of belonging.

Adapting to Circumstances: Whether using limited resources or catering to diverse dietary needs, flexibility and creativity are essential in making meals accessible and meaningful.

These insights are woven into the episodes of With Love, Meghan, where she demonstrates how viewers can apply these lessons in their own lives. Whether it's preparing a meal for a neighbor or volunteering at a local food bank, Meghan emphasizes that even small acts of kindness can have a ripple effect.

Transforming Meals into Acts of Love

For Meghan, every meal is an opportunity to express love and care. Whether it's a breakfast shared with her family or a potluck with friends, she believes in the transformative power of food to create connections and nurture relationships.

In this section, Meghan shares stories of how food has played a role in some of the most meaningful moments of her life. She recounts cooking with Harry for special occasions, baking banana bread for rural families in Australia during their royal tour, and preparing meals for evacuees during wildfires in California. Each story is a testament to how food can convey emotions that words often cannot.

Meghan also explores how meals can celebrate diversity and culture. She highlights recipes inspired by the many places she has called home, including California, Canada, and the United Kingdom. These dishes reflect her appreciation for different culinary traditions and the joy of sharing them with others.

Transforming meals into acts of love doesn't require grand gestures or expensive ingredients. In "With Love, Meghan," she demonstrates how even small touches—writing a heartfelt note to accompany a meal, setting the table thoughtfully, or simply asking someone how they're doing—can make a significant difference.

This chapter concludes with practical tips for turning everyday meals into meaningful experiences, such as:

Creating a welcoming atmosphere at the table.

Involving loved ones in the cooking process.

Being present and mindful during mealtime.

Through these stories and insights, Meghan invites viewers to view the kitchen as more than a space for cooking—it's a place to cultivate love, compassion, and connection, one meal at a time.

CHAPTER THREE

Beauty in the Garden

For Meghan, the garden is a sacred space—a place where life thrives, creativity blossoms, and peace can be found amidst chaos. In Montecito, where she and Prince Harry have built their home, the garden has become a refuge and a source of inspiration.

This chapter explores Meghan's journey of rediscovering nature, the profound healing power of gardening, and her commitment to sustainability. It highlights how tending to the earth can cultivate both physical beauty and emotional well-being, inspiring viewers to embrace nature in their own lives.

Rediscovering Nature in Montecito

Nestled in the serene hills of Montecito, Meghan's home is surrounded by lush greenery, vibrant flowers, and the tranquil sounds of nature. After years of a fast-paced lifestyle, the move to California allowed her to reconnect with the natural world in a deeply meaningful way.

Meghan describes her garden as a personal sanctuary—a space where she can slow down, reflect, and recharge. Whether planting flowers with her children, Archie and Lilibet, or enjoying a quiet moment with a cup of tea, she has come to appreciate the simple joys that nature provides.

In "With Love, Meghan," she shares how the garden has become a place of creativity and connection for her family. Together, they grow fruits, vegetables, and herbs, fostering an appreciation for where their food comes from and teaching the importance of nurturing the earth.

The garden also serves as a backdrop for meaningful conversations with friends and neighbors, reinforcing the idea that nature can bring people together.

Gardening for Mindfulness and Healing

Gardening has long been recognized as a therapeutic practice, and for Meghan, it has become an essential part of her self-care routine. In a world filled with constant distractions and pressures, the act of tending to plants offers a rare opportunity to be present and grounded.

Meghan speaks candidly about how gardening has helped her cope with stress and find clarity during challenging times. Pulling weeds, planting seeds, and watching plants grow serve as powerful metaphors for personal growth and resilience.

She encourages viewers to approach gardening not as a chore but as a mindful practice—one that fosters patience, gratitude, and a deeper connection to the world around them.

In this section, Meghan offers practical tips for incorporating gardening into daily life, even for those with limited space or experience. She demonstrates simple projects, such as creating a windowsill herb garden or planting pollinator-friendly flowers, that can bring the benefits of gardening to anyone.

Gardening is also presented as a communal activity. Meghan highlights how community gardens and shared green spaces can foster connections, promote inclusivity, and provide access to fresh, healthy food.

She shares inspiring stories of individuals and organizations using gardening to empower underserved communities and bring about positive change.

Sustainable Practices for Everyday Life

Meghan's commitment to sustainability is evident in her approach to gardening and beyond. She believes that small, intentional changes in our daily habits can have a significant impact on the environment. In With Love, Meghan, she shares practical strategies for making gardening—and life—more sustainable.

Some of her key sustainable practices include:

Composting: Meghan emphasizes the importance of reducing food waste by turning scraps into nutrient-rich compost for the garden.

Water Conservation: She demonstrates techniques such as drip irrigation, rainwater harvesting, and planting drought-resistant species to conserve water.

Choosing Native Plants: Meghan explains how native plants support local ecosystems, require less maintenance, and provide habitats for pollinators.

Reducing Chemical Use: Avoiding pesticides and synthetic fertilizers not only protects the environment but also ensures a healthier garden for families and wildlife.

Meghan also encourages viewers to think about sustainability in a broader context. From sourcing materials ethically to supporting local farmers and nurseries, every decision can contribute to a healthier planet.

She shares her philosophy that living sustainably is not about perfection but about making thoughtful, conscious choices that align with one's values.

This section concludes with a powerful message: that our relationship with the earth is a reciprocal one. By caring for nature, we are not only preserving its beauty for future generations but also enriching our own lives.

Meghan invites viewers to see their gardens—no matter how big or small—as spaces of hope, renewal, and possibility.

A Garden of Beauty and Meaning

Through her experiences in Montecito and her reflections on the healing and transformative power of gardening, Meghan inspires viewers to cultivate their own relationships with nature.

Whether planting a single flower or starting a vegetable garden, the act of nurturing life can bring beauty, peace, and purpose to our lives. In the words of Meghan, "The garden is a place where we can find ourselves and each other—a reminder that growth, connection, and beauty are always within reach."

CHAPTER FOUR

The Power of Conversation

In a world increasingly dominated by digital communication, the art of meaningful conversation remains a vital bridge between people. For Meghan, the power of dialogue lies in its ability to foster connection, inspire change, and build community.

This chapter delves into Meghan's personal experiences with heartfelt conversations, the transformative impact of storytelling, and her tips for hosting gatherings that encourage authentic connections.

Heartfelt Dialogues with Friends and Family

At the heart of Meghan's life are the deep, meaningful conversations she shares with her loved ones. These moments, whether over a quiet dinner or during a walk in nature, have strengthened her relationships and brought clarity to life's challenges.

Meghan believes that heartfelt dialogues are the foundation of connection. She often reflects on how simple, open-ended questions—like "How are you, really?"—can create space for vulnerability and understanding.

Whether discussing childhood memories with her mother, Doria, or navigating the complexities of public life with Prince

Harry, Meghan values honesty and empathy in every conversation.

In "With Love, Meghan," she shares personal anecdotes about conversations that shaped her perspective. One story recounts a late-night talk with Harry during a difficult time in their lives, which helped them find strength in each other and solidify their shared purpose.

Another highlights a heartwarming exchange with her son, Archie, who asked curious, innocent questions about the world around him, reminding her of the importance of listening with an open heart.

Meghan encourages viewers to prioritize quality time with their loved ones, suggesting practices like:

Creating Tech-Free Zones: Dedicate time to connect without the distractions of phones or screens.

Active Listening: Focus fully on the speaker, validating their feelings and experiences.

Sharing Gratitude: Take a moment to express appreciation for the people in your life.

Through these practices, Meghan demonstrates how meaningful conversations can nurture deeper bonds and bring joy and understanding into daily life.

How Stories Shape Communities

Stories are the threads that weave communities together, and Meghan understands the profound impact of sharing and listening to them. As a storyteller herself—whether through her acting career, public speaking, or charitable work—she has seen how narratives can inspire empathy, spark dialogue, and drive change.

Meghan often reflects on how her own story, shaped by her biracial identity and unique life journey, has helped her connect with people from diverse backgrounds. In With Love, Meghan, she emphasizes that everyone has a story worth sharing, no matter how ordinary it may seem.

This section explores the power of storytelling in building communities, including:

Empathy and Understanding: Listening to others' experiences broadens our perspectives and helps us find common ground.

Celebrating Diversity: Sharing stories from different cultures, traditions, and walks of life fosters inclusivity and appreciation.

Driving Social Change: Narratives have the power to challenge norms, break stigmas, and inspire collective action.

Meghan highlights examples of communities that have been transformed through storytelling, such as grassroots organizations that use personal narratives to advocate for policy change.

She also recounts powerful moments from her humanitarian work, where hearing someone's story often became the first step toward understanding their needs and finding solutions.

Through these insights, Meghan encourages viewers to embrace storytelling as a tool for connection and empowerment. Whether sharing their own experiences or listening to others, they can contribute to a more compassionate and united world.

Hosting Meaningful Gatherings

For Meghan, gatherings are more than social events—they are opportunities to create spaces where people feel valued, heard, and connected. Hosting has always been a natural extension of her belief in the power of conversation, and she shares her tips for organizing meaningful gatherings in "With Love, Meghan."

The Duchess approaches hosting with intention and thoughtfulness, ensuring that every detail contributes to an atmosphere of warmth and authenticity. Some of her key principles include:

Setting the Tone: Begin with a warm welcome and set an inclusive, positive vibe for the gathering.

Encouraging Dialogue: Arrange seating to promote conversation, and consider providing prompts or icebreakers to spark engagement.

Incorporating Personal Touches: Whether it's handwritten place cards or a playlist of favorite songs, small details make guests feel special.

Meghan also explores how gatherings can be a platform for deeper connections and shared purpose. She shares examples of intimate dinners where meaningful conversations about social justice and mental health took center stage, inspiring her and her guests to take action in their communities.

For viewers looking to host their own gatherings, Meghan offers practical advice:

Theme with Purpose: Consider organizing events around shared interests or causes, such as a book club, sustainability workshop, or community fundraiser.

Encourage Participation: Invite guests to contribute, whether by bringing a dish, sharing a story, or offering their perspective.

Focus on Presence: Create an environment where attendees feel comfortable being themselves and engaging fully.

By hosting with intention, Meghan believes we can transform gatherings into opportunities for genuine connection and lasting impact.

Celebrating the Power of Conversation

The chapter concludes with Meghan's reflections on the transformative power of dialogue. She emphasizes that conversations—whether between two people or within a community—are the foundation of understanding and progress.

Through heartfelt dialogues, the sharing of stories, and intentional gatherings, we can build bridges, celebrate diversity, and create spaces where everyone feels seen and valued.

In her words, "Every conversation has the potential to be a spark—a spark of connection, of understanding, of change. It all begins with listening and speaking from the heart."

CHAPTER FIVE

Creativity Through Adversity

Creativity often flourishes in the most unexpected moments, particularly during times of adversity. For Meghan, challenging periods in her life have been opportunities to explore her creativity, redefine her purpose, and find joy in small, meaningful acts.

This chapter explores how Meghan channels creativity as a tool for resilience and self-expression, offering insights into how others can do the same. From finding inspiration during hard times to engaging in soul-nourishing DIY projects, and ultimately turning setbacks into opportunities, Meghan's journey serves as a powerful reminder of the strength that lies within us all.

Finding Inspiration in Challenging Times

Adversity has a way of bringing clarity to what truly matters. For Meghan, life's challenges—both personal and public—have inspired her to tap into her creativity as a means of healing and growth. She shares candid reflections on moments when life's uncertainties pushed her to think outside the box and discover new ways to express herself.

One significant turning point in Meghan's life came when she transitioned from her acting career to her role as a global advocate and philanthropist.

This shift was not without its difficulties, but it sparked a period of reinvention, where Meghan found inspiration in her desire to create positive change.

She embraced writing, speaking, and community engagement as new forms of creative expression, channeling her passion for storytelling and connection.

In "With Love, Meghan," she emphasizes that creativity doesn't have to involve grand gestures or artistic talent. Instead, it can manifest in small, everyday actions—arranging flowers, journaling thoughts, or simply reimagining how to approach a problem.

Meghan encourages viewers to explore what brings them joy and to use those activities as a source of inspiration during tough times.

Her key advice includes:

Embrace the Process: Creativity is not about perfection but about exploration and self-discovery.

Find Joy in the Ordinary: Even mundane activities, like organizing a space or cooking a meal, can be creative outlets.

Let Challenges Fuel Innovation: Difficult circumstances often force us to think differently, leading to unexpected solutions and new opportunities.

Crafts and DIY Projects for the Soul

During moments of stress or uncertainty, Meghan turns to crafting and DIY projects as a form of self-care and mindfulness. These activities not only provide a creative outlet but also serve as a way to focus on the present moment and create something meaningful with her own hands.

In "With Love, Meghan," she shares some of her favorite DIY projects that are simple, accessible, and deeply rewarding. These include:

Personalized Gifts: Creating handmade cards or photo albums to celebrate special occasions and show appreciation for loved ones.

Home Décor Projects: Upcycling old furniture, making floral arrangements, or designing seasonal decorations to brighten up a space.

Nature-Inspired Crafts: Pressing flowers, making wreaths, or creating artwork using natural elements as a reminder of the beauty around us.

Meghan emphasizes that these projects don't have to be perfect to be meaningful. In fact, the imperfections often add character and authenticity to the final product. She encourages viewers to focus on the joy of creating rather than the outcome, reminding them that the process itself is a form of self-expression.

Crafting is also presented as a communal activity. Meghan highlights how working on DIY projects with family or friends can foster deeper connections and create lasting memories. She recounts heartwarming moments of crafting with her children, Archie and Lilibet, and how these activities have become cherished family traditions.

Turning Setbacks into Opportunities

Setbacks are an inevitable part of life, but Meghan views them as opportunities for growth and transformation. Drawing from her own experiences, she shares how moments of disappointment or failure have often led to new beginnings and greater clarity about her purpose.

One such instance was the decision to step back from royal duties and redefine her role as a public figure. While the transition was met with challenges, it also opened doors to new opportunities, such as launching Archewell, collaborating with organizations like World Central Kitchen, and creating projects like With Love, Meghan.

Each of these ventures allowed her to align her actions with her values and make a meaningful impact.

In this section, Meghan provides practical strategies for reframing setbacks as opportunities, including:

Adopting a Growth Mindset: Viewing challenges as learning experiences rather than obstacles.

Focusing on What You Can Control: Redirecting energy toward actions that align with your goals and values.

Celebrating Small Wins: Recognizing progress, no matter how small, helps maintain motivation and perspective.

She also discusses the importance of resilience and self-compassion during difficult times. By giving herself permission to pause, reflect, and heal, Meghan has been able to approach challenges with renewed strength and creativity.

Through personal stories and actionable advice, Meghan inspires viewers to see adversity as a catalyst for reinvention. She reminds them that setbacks are not the end of the story but rather an opportunity to write a new chapter—one filled with creativity, purpose, and possibility.

Embracing Creativity Through Adversity

This chapter concludes with Meghan's reflections on the transformative power of creativity. She encourages viewers to embrace life's challenges as opportunities to explore their creative potential and to find joy in the process of making, learning, and growing.

In her words, "Adversity can break us open in ways we never imagined, revealing the beauty and strength within us. When we embrace creativity, even in the hardest times, we create something beautiful—not just for ourselves but for the world around us."

CHAPTER SIX

Building Bridges, Not Walls

In an increasingly polarized world, Meghan believes in the power of building bridges that unite rather than walls that divide. This chapter delves into her philosophy of fostering inclusivity, collaboration, and understanding.

Drawing from her personal experiences, local initiatives, and global humanitarian efforts, Meghan demonstrates how diversity and cooperation can transform communities and inspire change.

Embracing Diversity in Community Efforts

Diversity is at the heart of any thriving community. Meghan's multicultural background and global experiences have shaped her deep appreciation for the richness that different perspectives bring to collective efforts.

She emphasizes that embracing diversity goes beyond acknowledging differences—it's about valuing them and ensuring everyone has a seat at the table.

In "With Love, Meghan," she reflects on her childhood in Los Angeles, where she was exposed to a tapestry of cultures and traditions. From her mother, Doria Ragland, she learned the importance of empathy and respect for others, regardless of their background.

These early lessons have influenced Meghan's approach to community building, which focuses on celebrating shared humanity while honoring individual identities.

Meghan highlights real-world examples of how diverse groups working together can lead to innovative solutions and stronger communities. She also shares practical ways viewers can promote inclusivity in their own efforts, such as:

Listening to Underrepresented Voices: Ensuring marginalized individuals have opportunities to share their stories and ideas.

Creating Safe Spaces: Building environments where people feel valued, respected, and empowered to contribute.

Learning and Unlearning: Actively seeking out new perspectives while challenging biases and assumptions.

Through these practices, Meghan inspires viewers to see diversity as a strength and a source of inspiration for collective action.

Collaborative Projects with Local Leaders

Meghan firmly believes in the power of local leadership. During her travels and philanthropic work, she has witnessed how grassroots initiatives driven by passionate individuals can create lasting change. This section highlights some of her most memorable collaborations with local leaders and the lessons she has learned from these experiences.

One poignant story Meghan shares is her involvement with a women's collective in South Africa during her royal tour in 2019. The group, focused on empowering women through sustainable employment, left a profound impact on Meghan.

She recounts how the collective's founder, a local community leader, used limited resources to build an initiative that provided dignity and opportunity to countless women.

Meghan also reflects on her partnerships with community organizations in California, where she has worked alongside local leaders to address pressing issues like food insecurity and disaster relief.

From distributing meals to wildfire evacuees to donating supplies to underfunded schools, these projects underscore her belief that meaningful change often begins at the local level.

Key takeaways from Meghan's collaborative efforts include:

Building Trust: Authentic partnerships require mutual respect, transparency, and a shared commitment to the cause.

Amplifying Local Voices: Recognizing that those closest to the issues are often best equipped to lead the solutions.

Leveraging Resources: Using one's platform or connections to support and elevate local initiatives.

Through these examples, Meghan emphasizes the importance of coming together with humility and a willingness to learn, reminding viewers that impactful change is a collective effort.

Lessons from Working with Global Organizations

Meghan's work with international organizations has given her a global perspective on community building and social impact.

From her role as a UN Women advocate to her collaborations with World Central Kitchen and other NGOs, she has seen firsthand how global efforts can address systemic challenges while fostering cross-cultural understanding.

In "With Love, Meghan," she reflects on her time working with the UN, where she championed gender equality and women's empowerment. She recounts a pivotal moment during a visit to Rwanda, where she met women rebuilding their lives after conflict.

Their resilience and determination inspired Meghan to deepen her commitment to advocating for marginalized communities worldwide.

Meghan also highlights her partnership with World Central Kitchen (WCK), an organization that provides meals to communities in crisis. Collaborating with WCK founder José Andrés, she has supported their mission to deliver food and hope in the aftermath of natural disasters and humanitarian emergencies.

Key lessons from Meghan's global work include:

The Importance of Cultural Sensitivity: Understanding and respecting local customs and practices is essential for effective collaboration.

Adapting to Local Needs: Tailoring solutions to the unique challenges and strengths of each community ensures sustainable impact.

Fostering Global Solidarity: Recognizing that global challenges, such as climate change and inequality, require collective action and shared responsibility.

Meghan encourages viewers to think globally while acting locally, reminding them that small, intentional actions in their own communities can contribute to broader positive change.

A World United Through Collaboration

The chapter concludes with Meghan's reflections on the power of unity and cooperation. She emphasizes that building bridges—whether between individuals, communities, or nations—requires courage, empathy, and a willingness to embrace our shared humanity.

In her words, "When we come together with open hearts and minds, we create a world where everyone has the opportunity to thrive. By building bridges instead of walls, we not only connect with others but also discover the best within ourselves."

This chapter serves as a call to action for viewers to embrace diversity, collaborate with others, and work toward a more inclusive and united future.

CHAPTER SEVEN

Acts of Kindness

Acts of kindness, no matter how small, have the power to create ripples of positivity that can transform lives and strengthen communities. Meghan firmly believes in the importance of living a life rooted in compassion and generosity, and she emphasizes that kindness is a choice we can make every day.

This chapter explores the profound impact of small gestures, purposeful volunteering, and raising children with compassion at their core.

Small Gestures That Make Big Differences

While grand gestures of charity often capture headlines, Meghan reminds us that it's the small, everyday acts of kindness that often make the most profound impact. From offering a kind word to a stranger to writing a heartfelt note to a friend, these simple actions can brighten someone's day and foster a culture of care and connection.

Meghan shares personal stories of small acts of kindness that have stayed with her. One touching memory is of a stranger who comforted her during a particularly challenging moment in her early acting career. Their empathy reminded her of the importance of being there for others, even in seemingly insignificant ways.

In With Love, Meghan, she provides practical ideas for small acts of kindness, including:

Leaving Encouraging Notes: Writing uplifting messages and leaving them in public places, such as libraries or coffee shops.

Offering Help: Assisting someone with groceries, holding open a door, or helping a neighbor with a task.

Spreading Positivity Online: Sharing supportive comments or uplifting posts on social media to counter negativity.

Meghan emphasizes that these gestures don't require significant time or resources—they simply require intention. She encourages viewers to look for opportunities to be kind in their everyday lives, reminding them that even the smallest action can make a big difference.

Volunteering with Purpose

Volunteering has always been a cornerstone of Meghan's life. From her early days of serving meals at soup kitchens in Los Angeles to her current work with organizations like World Central Kitchen, Meghan has seen how giving time and effort can create lasting impact.

In this section, she reflects on the importance of volunteering with purpose and offers guidance on how to get involved in meaningful ways.

Meghan shares a deeply personal story about volunteering with Prince Harry at a food bank in the UK. The experience not only strengthened their bond but also reinforced her belief in the importance of showing up for others.

She recalls the gratitude expressed by those they served, which underscored the value of even the smallest contribution.

To help viewers find their own paths to purposeful volunteering, Meghan offers these tips:

Align with Your Passions: Choose causes that resonate with your values and interests, whether it's education, the environment, or social justice.

Start Local: Look for opportunities within your community, such as mentoring programs, clean-up initiatives, or animal shelters.

Commit Consistently: Even small, regular contributions of time can have a significant impact over the long term.

Meghan also highlights how volunteering benefits not only the recipients but also the volunteers themselves. It fosters a sense of purpose, builds connections, and provides opportunities for personal growth.

Encouraging Compassion in Children

One of Meghan's greatest joys as a mother is instilling values of kindness and empathy in her children, Archie and Lilibet. She believes that teaching compassion at a young age sets the foundation for a lifetime of meaningful relationships and positive contributions to society.

In this section, Meghan shares how she and Prince Harry encourage their children to practice kindness in their daily lives. From simple activities, like making thank-you cards for their teachers, to involving them in charitable initiatives, they strive to show their children that every act of kindness matters.

Meghan offers practical suggestions for parents who want to nurture compassion in their children:

Lead by Example: Children learn by watching the adults in their lives, so demonstrate kindness in your words and actions.

Practice Gratitude: Encourage kids to express appreciation for what they have and to consider how they can help others.

Foster Empathy: Read books or share stories that highlight diverse perspectives and experiences to help children understand and appreciate others.

She also emphasizes the importance of creating opportunities for children to give back. Whether it's organizing a neighborhood toy drive or participating in a community service project, involving children in acts of kindness helps them develop a sense of responsibility and purpose.

Meghan shares a heartwarming anecdote about Archie's first experience donating toys to children in need. She recalls his excitement and pride in knowing he was helping others, a moment that reaffirmed her commitment to raising compassionate, socially conscious children.

Kindness as a Way of Life

This chapter concludes with Meghan's reflections on the transformative power of kindness. She underscores that acts of kindness—whether big or small—have the ability to bridge divides, heal wounds, and create a ripple effect of positivity.

In her words, "Kindness is not just something we do; it's a way of being. It's the simplest, yet most profound way to remind ourselves and others of our shared humanity. When we choose kindness, we create a better world—not only for ourselves but for generations to come."

Through this chapter, Meghan invites viewers to embrace kindness as a guiding principle in their lives and to inspire others, especially children, to do the same.

CHAPTER EIGHT

Living with Intentionality

Living intentionally means aligning one's actions with one's values, beliefs, and goals. In this chapter, Meghan invites viewers to explore the power of intentionality in everyday life—whether it's creating a home that fosters peace and purpose, simplifying daily routines to find deeper fulfillment, or embracing conscious consumerism to make mindful choices.

Meghan's journey toward intentional living is rooted in her desire to live authentically and purposefully. Through personal stories and actionable advice, she encourages others to reflect on their own lives and make decisions that align with what truly matters.

Designing a Home That Reflects Your Values

For Meghan, home is more than just a physical space—it is a sanctuary that reflects her values, personality, and vision for the future. She believes that the environment we create for ourselves should support our well-being, foster creativity, and encourage mindfulness.

In this section, Meghan takes viewers on a journey through her own approach to home design, offering insights on how to curate spaces that feel both authentic and harmonious.

Meghan's home in Montecito, California, which she shares with Prince Harry and their children, serves as an example of how intentional living can be woven into the fabric of daily life.

She describes how the design choices they made—from sustainable materials to art that resonates with them personally—reflect their commitment to creating an environment of comfort, warmth, and connection. Meghan emphasizes that home design should be a reflection of who you are, not who you think you should be.

In With Love, Meghan, she provides practical tips for creating a home that embodies your values, including:

Incorporate Personal Touches: Display meaningful objects, photographs, and artwork that tell your story and evoke positive memories.

Create Functional Spaces: Designate spaces for relaxation, creativity, and connection to align with your daily activities and emotional needs.

Choose Sustainability: Make mindful choices in furnishings, decor, and materials that reflect a commitment to the environment, such as using eco-friendly fabrics or opting for locally sourced items.

Meghan also highlights the importance of cultivating a sense of peace and mindfulness within the home. She shares how small rituals, like lighting a candle or taking a moment of silence before a meal, can create an atmosphere of calm and gratitude.

Simplifying Life for Greater Fulfillment

In a world that constantly pulls us in multiple directions, simplifying life is a powerful way to reclaim time, energy, and peace of mind. Meghan shares her personal journey of reducing the clutter—both physical and mental—that can sometimes overwhelm our lives. By focusing on what truly matters and letting go of distractions, she has found greater fulfillment and clarity.

Meghan reflects on how her approach to simplicity has evolved over the years. As she transitioned from her high-profile career in acting to her philanthropic work, she realized that a simpler, more focused lifestyle allowed her to be more present and intentional in her relationships and endeavors.

In "With Love, Meghan," she offers viewers practical advice on simplifying life, including:

Decluttering Your Physical Space: Letting go of unnecessary possessions to create a more organized and peaceful environment. Meghan discusses the power of minimalism in fostering a sense of freedom and space.

Streamlining Your Schedule: Reducing commitments and learning to say no to activities that don't align with your values or goals. Meghan encourages viewers to prioritize quality over quantity when it comes to how they spend their time.

Cultivating Mental Clarity: Practicing mindfulness and journaling to clear the mind of unnecessary stress, helping to create space for new ideas and deeper connections.

Meghan believes that simplifying life doesn't mean sacrificing joy or experiences—it means making room for the things that truly bring fulfillment and alignment with one's purpose.

The Joy of Conscious Consumerism

Conscious consumerism is about making intentional purchasing decisions that reflect your values—whether that's supporting ethical brands, reducing waste, or choosing products that contribute to the well-being of people and the planet.

Meghan shares how she has become more mindful of the impact her purchases have on the world and how others can do the same.

In her own life, Meghan has taken steps to reduce her environmental footprint by choosing sustainable fashion, supporting companies with ethical labor practices, and making eco-friendly choices for her family. She believes that every purchase is an opportunity to vote for the kind of world we want to live in.

Meghan encourages viewers to embrace conscious consumerism by considering the following principles:

Support Ethical Brands: Look for companies that prioritize fair labor practices, sustainability, and transparency. Meghan highlights some of her favorite brands that align with these values, such as those that create fashion from recycled materials or prioritize eco-friendly packaging.

Invest in Quality Over Quantity: Instead of purchasing fast fashion or disposable items, Meghan advocates for buying fewer, but higher-quality products that last longer and are made with care.

Reduce, Reuse, Recycle: Make environmentally friendly choices by reducing waste, repurposing items, and supporting the circular economy. Meghan discusses the importance of buying second-hand, donating gently used items, and embracing sustainable fashion practices.

Meghan also reflects on how living consciously extends beyond material goods. It involves how we consume information, how we interact with others, and how we engage with the world. By adopting a holistic approach to conscious consumerism, Meghan believes we can create a world where our choices reflect the values of kindness, sustainability, and social responsibility.

Living with Intention: A Path to Fulfillment

This chapter concludes with Meghan's reflections on how living with intentionality leads to a deeper sense of purpose and fulfillment. She encourages viewers to create lives that reflect their deepest values, whether through their homes, daily habits, or purchasing choices.

In her words, "When we live with intention, we create the space for joy, peace, and fulfillment to thrive. We don't just exist—we create lives that are meaningful, purposeful, and deeply connected to the world around us."

Meghan reminds viewers that intentionality is a lifelong practice that requires mindfulness, reflection, and commitment, but the rewards are immeasurable. By making conscious choices, we align ourselves with our true purpose, creating a life that is both fulfilling and aligned with our deepest values.

CHAPTER NINE

Finding Strength in Vulnerability

In this chapter, Meghan explores the transformative power of vulnerability and how embracing our authentic selves—especially in the face of adversity—can foster deeper connections, build resilience, and empower others.

Vulnerability is often viewed as a weakness, but Meghan demonstrates that it is, in fact, one of the greatest sources of strength. By opening up about her own experiences of public scrutiny, personal struggles, and moments of self-doubt, Meghan shows how vulnerability can lead to healing, growth, and connection.

The Role of Authenticity in Building Relationships

Authenticity is the foundation of meaningful relationships. Meghan discusses how being true to oneself and allowing others to see both the strengths and imperfections in our lives is crucial to forming lasting and genuine connections. She reflects on the importance of transparency and vulnerability in both her personal and professional relationships.

Throughout her journey, Meghan has learned that hiding behind a mask of perfection or trying to meet others' expectations only leads to isolation and disconnection. She shares that her most fulfilling relationships have been the ones where both she and others have been free to express their authentic selves.

In "With Love, Meghan," Meghan offers insights on how to build authentic relationships, including:

Embrace Imperfection: Meghan explains that it's okay to show vulnerability, as it humanizes us and makes us more relatable. She shares how allowing herself to be imperfect has deepened her relationships with her family, friends, and even the public.

Listen with Compassion: Building authentic connections requires not only speaking from the heart but also listening with empathy. Meghan highlights the importance of truly hearing and understanding others without judgment.

Be Transparent About Needs and Boundaries: Meghan shares how, in her own relationships, being clear about her needs and setting healthy boundaries has fostered mutual respect and trust.

Meghan emphasizes that authenticity doesn't mean being constantly open about every aspect of one's life—it's about being true to your core values and not hiding behind a facade. When we embrace who we are, we allow others to do the same.

Overcoming Public Scrutiny and Criticism

As a public figure, Meghan has faced intense scrutiny and criticism throughout her life. From her early days as an actress to her time as a member of the British royal family and beyond, she has been constantly under the microscope of the media and public opinion.

Rather than retreating from this scrutiny, Meghan has chosen to confront it head-on, embracing vulnerability as a means of personal strength.

In this section, Meghan shares her experience of navigating public criticism and finding her voice in the face of it. She discusses the emotional toll that constant judgment can have on one's mental health but also reveals how vulnerability can serve as a powerful tool for resilience and healing.

Meghan opens up about the challenges she faced as a new member of the royal family, especially the media's portrayal of her and the pressures that came with the role. She recalls how the public's harsh opinions often weighed heavily on her, leading her to question her own worth and identity.

Yet, over time, she learned to confront these external judgments and focus on what truly mattered to her—her family, her values, and her personal well-being.

In "With Love, Meghan," she shares strategies for dealing with public scrutiny and criticism:

Focus on Your Truth: Meghan emphasizes that staying true to one's core beliefs is essential when facing public criticism. She discusses how, by reaffirming her own sense of identity and purpose, she was able to rise above the negativity.

Seek Support from Loved Ones: Meghan highlights the importance of having a solid support network. She shares how, during difficult times, she leaned on her close family and friends to help her navigate the challenges of public life.

Engage with Compassion, Not Defensiveness: While it's tempting to respond defensively to criticism, Meghan urges viewers to meet negativity with grace and understanding, rather than reacting impulsively.

Meghan's journey of overcoming public scrutiny shows that vulnerability is not a sign of weakness—it is a sign of strength and courage. By allowing herself to be vulnerable, she has learned to reclaim her narrative and find peace in her truth.

Sharing Stories to Empower Others

Meghan has always believed in the power of storytelling. She views storytelling as a means of connection, healing, and empowerment.

By sharing her own experiences—both the joys and the struggles—she has been able to create a space for others to share their own stories and find solidarity. Meghan's openness has inspired countless individuals, showing them that they are not alone in their struggles.

In this section, Meghan discusses how sharing stories can be a tool for empowering others, particularly those who may feel marginalized or voiceless. She reflects on the transformative impact that storytelling can have in breaking down barriers, challenging stereotypes, and fostering understanding.

One of Meghan's most powerful storytelling moments was her candid discussion about her miscarriage, which she shared in an op-ed for The New York Times. She recalls how the experience of writing about her loss was both cathartic and healing for her, but it also resonated deeply with others who had experienced similar pain.

Meghan's vulnerability in sharing this deeply personal story allowed her to connect with people on a profound level and encouraged others to share their own experiences of grief and healing.

Meghan encourages others to share their stories, not only for their own healing but to create a ripple effect of understanding and empowerment. She shares the following advice:

Embrace Your Story: Everyone's story is valuable, and sharing it can help others feel seen and heard. Meghan reminds viewers that they are not alone in their experiences.

Be Honest About Your Struggles: Vulnerability can inspire others to speak their truth. Meghan urges people to share not just their successes but their struggles as well, as they often carry the greatest lessons and insights.

Create Safe Spaces for Others: When we share our stories, we create a space for others to do the same. Meghan encourages viewers to foster environments—whether online, in the workplace, or in their personal lives—where people feel safe to express their own vulnerabilities.

Through sharing her story, Meghan has empowered countless individuals to embrace their own vulnerability and find strength in their truths. She firmly believes that when we share our experiences, we create a culture of compassion, healing, and empowerment.

Vulnerability as Empowerment

The chapter concludes with Meghan's reflections on how embracing vulnerability has been one of the greatest sources of strength in her life. She emphasizes that vulnerability is not a sign of fragility; rather, it is a powerful tool for connection, healing, and empowerment.

In her words, "When we allow ourselves to be vulnerable, we open the door to deep connection, both with ourselves and with others. It's in our shared stories, our shared pain, and our shared joy that we truly find our strength."

Meghan invites viewers to reframe vulnerability as a source of empowerment rather than weakness. By embracing their true selves, sharing their stories, and confronting public criticism with grace, they can find strength, resilience, and a deeper connection with those around them.

CHAPTER TEN

Celebrating the Unexpected

In this chapter of "With Love, Meghan," the Duchess of Sussex explores the transformative power of embracing the unexpected, especially during challenging times. Life is full of surprises—some joyful, others difficult—but Meghan shows that when we learn to approach life's uncertainties with an open heart and mind, we can transform challenges into moments of celebration.

By fostering a mindset of gratitude and hope, we can navigate life's twists and turns with optimism and resilience. Meghan reflects on her own experiences and the lessons she has learned from turning adversity into opportunities for growth and celebration.

Transforming Challenges into Celebrations

Life's unexpected challenges are inevitable, but Meghan believes that how we choose to respond to these challenges defines us. Instead of allowing hardships to define our experiences negatively, she advocates for finding moments of celebration even in the face of adversity. For Meghan, celebrating the unexpected means finding joy in life's surprises, no matter how difficult they may seem at first.

Throughout her journey, Meghan has faced numerous public and personal challenges—from her early career in

Hollywood to her transition into royal life, and later, the intense media scrutiny she faced after stepping back from royal duties.

Each of these challenges presented an opportunity for growth and reinvention. Meghan reflects on how these moments, which initially felt like setbacks, eventually led her to a greater understanding of herself, her family, and her values.

In this section, Meghan shares personal anecdotes about how she has reframed challenges in her own life:

Find the Silver Lining: Meghan encourages viewers to look for the lessons in difficult situations. For example, the decision to step away from royal duties, although controversial, allowed her to take control of her narrative and pursue her passion for social justice work.

Celebrate Small Wins: While major milestones are worth celebrating, Meghan stresses the importance of acknowledging and appreciating small victories along the way. Whether it's making a difficult decision or simply getting through a challenging day, each step forward deserves recognition.

Embrace Growth Through Change: Change is often uncomfortable, but it is also the source of growth. Meghan explains how she learned to embrace change, knowing that it often opens doors to new opportunities and perspectives.

By transforming obstacles into moments of reflection, gratitude, and celebration, Meghan demonstrates that challenges can be powerful catalysts for positive change, leading to unexpected and beautiful outcomes.

Gratitude as a Daily Practice

Gratitude has long been recognized as one of the most powerful tools for fostering happiness, resilience, and well-being. In this section, Meghan discusses how incorporating gratitude into her daily routine has helped her maintain perspective, even during difficult times.

She believes that cultivating a gratitude practice allows us to shift our focus from what's missing in our lives to what is abundant, fostering a sense of contentment and joy.

Meghan recalls how, during some of her most challenging moments, she turned to gratitude as a grounding practice. Whether dealing with public criticism or personal loss, she found that taking time each day to reflect on what she was grateful for helped her maintain a sense of peace and clarity.

In "With Love, Meghan," she shares tips on how to integrate gratitude into daily life:

Start Each Day with Gratitude: Meghan suggests beginning the day with a moment of reflection, naming at least three things you're grateful for. This simple practice can set a positive tone for the day ahead.

Gratitude Journaling: Meghan encourages viewers to keep a gratitude journal, where they can jot down moments, people, or experiences that bring them joy and appreciation. Writing down these reflections helps anchor the practice and make it more intentional.

Express Gratitude to Others: Meghan emphasizes the importance of sharing gratitude with those around us. She describes how expressing thanks to her family, friends, and even colleagues helps nurture stronger relationships and creates a cycle of positivity.

Meghan highlights that gratitude is not about ignoring life's challenges but about recognizing the blessings, even in the midst of difficulty. She believes that by focusing on the positive, we create space for more joy and fulfillment to enter our lives.

Living with Hope and Optimism

Hope and optimism are powerful forces that can guide us through life's uncertainties. Meghan discusses how cultivating a hopeful mindset has been a key factor in her ability to navigate challenges with resilience and grace. She reflects on how, despite facing significant obstacles, she has always held on to the belief that positive change is possible—and that the best is yet to come.

For Meghan, hope is not about blind optimism or denying life's hardships. Instead, it is about trusting that, no matter what happens, we have the strength and capacity to overcome adversity and grow. It is a belief that, even in the darkest times, there is light ahead.

In this section, Meghan shares how she stays hopeful and optimistic, even in the face of difficulty:

Focus on What You Can Control: Meghan emphasizes the importance of focusing on the aspects of life we can control, such as our responses, actions, and mindset. By letting go of what's beyond our control, we free ourselves to make positive choices in the present moment.

Surround Yourself with Positivity: Meghan talks about how the people we surround ourselves with can have a profound impact on our mindset. She stresses the importance of building a supportive network of friends and family who uplift and inspire us.

Practice Self-Compassion: Hope can only flourish when we are kind and compassionate with ourselves. Meghan shares how, during times of personal struggle, she learned to offer herself the same kindness and understanding that she would offer to a loved one.

Through her own journey, Meghan has learned that hope is not passive—it is an active practice that requires intentionality and resilience. By nurturing hope and optimism, we are better equipped to navigate life's challenges and embrace the opportunities that arise from them.

Celebrating the Unexpected: A Life of Gratitude, Hope, and Joy

The chapter concludes with Meghan's reflections on the importance of celebrating the unexpected. By embracing life's uncertainties with a heart full of gratitude and hope, we open ourselves up to the possibility of transformation, growth, and unexpected blessings.

Meghan encourages viewers to cultivate a mindset that celebrates both the good and the challenging moments, as each experience offers valuable lessons and opportunities for connection.

In her words, "When we learn to embrace the unexpected, we not only find joy in the journey but also unlock the true magic of life. Each challenge is an opportunity to grow, and each unexpected twist is an invitation to celebrate the beauty of the unknown."

Meghan's message is clear: life is a journey of continuous growth, and by living with gratitude, hope, and optimism, we can turn every experience—whether joyous or difficult—into an opportunity to celebrate.

CONCLUSION

A Call to Action: Spreading Compassion and Creativity

As “With Love, Meghan” draws to a close, the Duchess of Sussex reflects on the profound journey of compassion, creativity, and community that she has shared throughout the series.

From the kitchen to the garden, from conversations to acts of kindness, each chapter has underscored a core belief: that the unexpected moments of life, when embraced with an open heart and mind, hold the power to transform not only our lives but also the lives of those around us.

Meghan's vision for the series has been clear: to inspire viewers to cultivate a life of intentionality, to find beauty even in the midst of challenges, and to spread love through acts of kindness, creativity, and compassion.

In the final moments of "With Love, Meghan," the Duchess leaves viewers with a powerful call to action. The world is full of challenges, both personal and collective, but it is also full of opportunities for change and growth.

Meghan encourages everyone—regardless of background or circumstance—to embrace compassion, creativity, and community as guiding principles in their everyday lives.

She emphasizes that the act of spreading compassion does not need to be grandiose or elaborate. It can start with small, everyday gestures that have the power to ripple outward, touching the lives of others in meaningful ways.

Whether it's through a thoughtful conversation, a simple meal shared with a neighbor, or offering help to those in need, Meghan believes that compassion is contagious, and by showing kindness to others, we can inspire a wave of positivity in the world.

Creativity, too, plays an integral role in creating positive change. Meghan encourages viewers to embrace their creative instincts, whether they manifest in the kitchen, the garden, or in more artistic endeavors.

Creativity allows us to connect with others, express our emotions, and reframe challenges in ways that lead to growth and healing. By nurturing our creativity and sharing it with others, we contribute to a world that values self-expression and innovation.

In her closing remarks, Meghan invites viewers to take what they have learned throughout the series and apply it to their own lives, making a commitment to spread compassion and creativity wherever they go.

She shares that it is through these acts of kindness and creativity that we can build stronger communities, foster deeper connections, and transform the world into a more beautiful and supportive place for all.

Meghan's Reflections on the Journey

As the series comes to an end, Meghan takes a moment to reflect on her own personal growth and the transformative journey she has experienced throughout the process of creating With Love, Meghan.

The project has allowed her to share pieces of herself with the world in ways she hadn't imagined, and in doing so, she has come to understand more deeply the importance of staying true to her values, embracing vulnerability, and continuously seeking ways to serve others.

Meghan reflects on how the act of creating the series itself was a journey of self-discovery. She shares how, in opening up about her passions—whether that's cooking, gardening, or humanitarian work—she was able to connect more deeply with her audience.

More importantly, she learned how to approach each aspect of her life with an open heart, finding beauty in moments both big and small. Through the ups and downs of her personal life, Meghan has learned that embracing vulnerability and staying authentic to her beliefs is not only empowering for herself but also deeply enriching for others.

She acknowledges that there have been difficult times, where public criticism, personal loss, and family challenges seemed overwhelming. However, it was in those very moments that she learned the power of love, both given and received, and how moments of adversity often hold the greatest potential for growth and renewal.

In her reflections, Meghan shares:

On Empathy: "What I have come to realize is that the more we give of ourselves in empathy and understanding, the more we receive in return. Empathy is a language we all understand, no matter where we come from."

On Creativity: “Creativity is freedom. It’s about unlocking something within us that transcends words, whether through art, food, or community-building. Creativity is a healing force that brings us closer to each other.”

On Compassion: “Compassion is the heartbeat of humanity. It is our ability to see each other not as strangers but as reflections of ourselves. When we approach each other with compassion, we pave the way for a world full of possibility.”

Meghan encourages viewers to never underestimate the power of their own journeys. She believes that every person has the potential to make a positive impact on the world, no matter how small the action may seem. It's through the collective efforts of compassionate and creative individuals that true change occurs.

Embracing Beauty in Every Moment

The final message of "With Love, Meghan" is a celebration of beauty in every moment—whether it's found in quiet reflection, in the simple act of sharing a meal, or in the courage to speak one's truth.

Meghan invites her audience to embrace life with a sense of wonder and gratitude, to see the beauty in both the ordinary and the extraordinary. By recognizing the inherent beauty in our daily lives and the world around us, we can shift our perspective and find joy even in the most challenging circumstances.

She reminds viewers that beauty is not just something we see with our eyes, but something we feel in our hearts. It's in the connection we share with others, the love we offer, and the creativity we express.

It's in the moments of quiet reflection and the ways we respond to life's uncertainties. Meghan believes that when we open ourselves to the beauty in every moment, we create space for joy, healing, and transformation.

In her final reflection, Meghan encourages all to take a moment each day to pause and appreciate the small things—the laughter of loved ones, the warmth of the sun, the simplicity of a home-cooked meal. These seemingly ordinary moments are, in fact, where the true beauty of life resides.

Her message is clear: "The beauty of life lies not in perfection but in our ability to find joy, love, and connection in the most unexpected moments. We are all part of this beautiful, messy, and extraordinary journey. And when we embrace it fully—with love, compassion, and creativity—we can truly make a difference."

In this way, Meghan closes the chapter and the series, inviting her viewers to live intentionally, with gratitude and optimism, and to always embrace beauty in every moment—no matter how unexpected or imperfect.